MODERN ERAS · UNCOVERED ·

the mid
1930s
to
1945

# From Jesse Owens to Hiroshima

KINGSTON UPON HULL
CITY LIBRARIES

## Sean Sheehan

# www.raintreepublishers.co.uk

Visit our website to find out more information about **Raintree** books.

To order:

☎ Phone 44 (0) 1865 888113

📄 Send a fax to 44 (0) 1865 314091

💻 Visit the Raintree Bookshop at **www.raintreepublishers.co.uk** to browse our catalogue and order online.

First published in Great Britain by Raintree, Halley Court, Jordan Hill, Oxford, OX2 8EJ, part of Harcourt Education.
Raintree is a registered trademark of Harcourt Education Ltd.

© Harcourt Education Ltd 2006
First published in paperback 2007
The moral right of the proprietor has been asserted.

Editorial: Melanie Copland, Tameika Martin, and Lucy Beevor
Design: Michelle Lisseter and Bridge Creatives Services Ltd
Picture Research: Mica Brancic and Ginny Stroud-Lewis
Production: Duncan Gilbert

Originated by Chroma Graphics (Overseas) Pte. Ltd
Printed and bound in China by South China Printing Company

10 digit ISBN 1 844 43952 6 (hardback)
13 digit ISBN 978 1 844 43952 2 (hardback)
10 09 08 07 06
10 9 8 7 6 5 4 3 2 1
10 digit ISBN 1 844 43962 3 (paperback)
13 digit ISBN 978 1 844 43962 1 (paperback)
10 09 08 07 06
10 9 8 7 6 5 4 3 2 1

British Library Cataloguing in Publication Data
Sheehan, Sean
From Jessie Owens to Hiroshima. – (Modern Eras Uncovered)
909.8'23
A full catalogue record for this book is available from the British Library.

**Acknowledgements**
Corbis p. **21, 30, 37, 40, 44, 45**; Corbis/Seattle Post-Intelligencer Collection/Museum of History & Industry p. **35**; Corbis/Bettmann pp. **4, 7, 8, 14, 19, 20, 23, 32, 43** (bottom), **46, 47**; Corbis/Hulton-Deutsch Collection p. **15**; Getty Images p. **33**; Getty Images/Hulton Archive pp. **6, 9, 10, 11, 25, 26, 34, 36, 38, 42, 48, 49**; Getty Images/Time Life Pictures pp. **31, 43** (middle); The Advertising Archive Ltd p. **12**; The Bridgeman Art Library/Museo Nacional Centro de Arte Reina Sofia, Madrid, Spain © Succession Picasso/DACS 2004 p. **16/17**; The Bridgeman Art Library/Private Collection p. **13**; The Novosti Press Agency p. **39**.

Cover photograph (top) reproduced with permission of Corbis/Bettman, and photograph (bottom) reproduced with permission of Corbis.

I GET A KICK OUT OF YOU
Words and Music by Cole Porter
© 1934 (Renewed) Harms Inc, USA
Chappell Music Ltd, London W6 8BS
Reproduced by permission of International Music Publications Ltd.
All Rights Reserved.

# CONTENTS

Any words appearing in the text in bold, **like this**, are explained in the glossary.

# TROUBLED TIMES

The Olympic Games are supposed to celebrate **internationalism** and friendly competition through sport. In 1896, when the Olympic Games were held for the first time since the days of ancient Greece, only 14 countries and 241 male athletes took part. By 1936, when the Games were held in Berlin, Germany, nearly 50 countries were represented and nearly 4,000 male and female athletes took part. Sport and leisure activities were becoming increasingly popular. The Berlin Olympics also saw politics and racism affecting sports in a major way for the first time. Hitler, the ruler of Germany, was a racist who believed white people were a superior race. The victory of an African-American athlete, Jessie Owens, in the 100 metre race was not what he expected.

The Olympic flame finally reaches the *Lustgarten* in Berlin, Germany, signalling the start of the 9th Olympic Games on 7 August 1936.

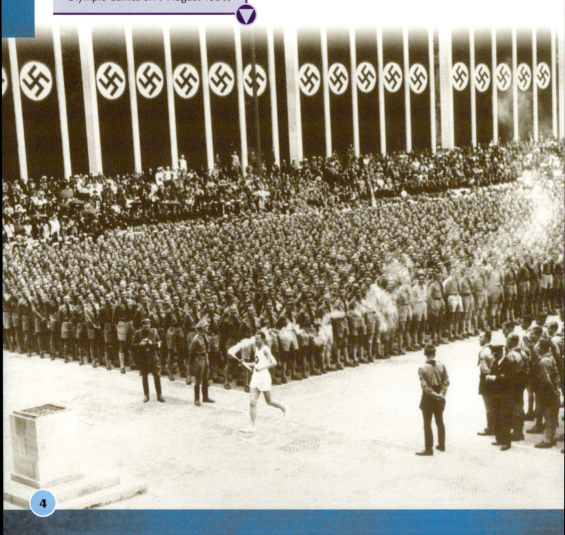

Hitler wanted power and the creation of a racist state not only in Germany, but across the whole of Europe. This led to the outbreak of the Second World War in 1939. Two years later, with the attack on Pearl Harbor by the Japanese, the United States was brought into the war. The Second World War lasted until 1945 and only then did the full horror of **Nazism** become known to the world. After 1945, the world also had to live with the fact that an extremely powerful new type of weapon, based on splitting an **atom** and releasing its energy, had come into being.

The Second World War was the most destructive war in history. It killed more people than any other war before or since. It dominated the period between 1936 and the end of the war in 1945. The end of the war did, however, see the defeat of Nazism and of the German and Japanese **empires**. It also produced a world dominated by two superpowers, the United States and the **USSR**.

## Military spending

The world became dominated by the needs of war between 1939 and 1945, and military spending quickly rose. By 1945, the United States and the USSR had become more powerful than other countries.

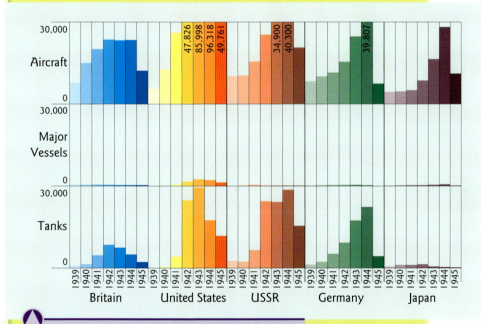

This chart shows how much the military spending of Britain, United States, the USSR, Germany, and Japan increased during the Second World War.

# BEFORE THE WAR

In the UK, in the years before the war broke out, there was dramatic news on the radio and in the newspapers. In 1934, passenger flights between Australia and the UK were introduced for the first time. The following year, Malcolm Campbell became the first man in a vehicle, called *Bluebird*, to exceed 300 miles (482 kilometres) per hour on land. In 1936, the BBC made its first regular television broadcasts. In London and other major cities, better-off families were moving from the crowded city centres to **suburbs** where new houses were being built. Only people who paid attention to foreign news had reason to worry about the possibility of another war in Europe.

## Hitler rules Germany

After becoming the leader of Germany in 1933, Hitler set up a **totalitarian** government. This type of government can do whatever it likes and no opposition is allowed. Hitler became a **dictator**, and declared himself the leader – *der Führer*. He set about imprisoning people who might dare to oppose him.

## Attacking Jews

One group of people that Hitler began to attack, or **persecute**, were Jews. Jews that worked for the government, including teachers, lost their jobs. Jewish actors were banned from performing, and it became illegal to publicly show or sell Jewish newspapers. The mass burning of Jewish books was organized. In 1935, Jews lost their German citizenship, and marriages between Jews and non-Jews were forbidden.

This Jewish woman sits on a park bench in Nazi Germany around 1938. The bench is marked "Nur für Juden!" (For Jews only).

In 1938, on the night of 9 November, Jewish buildings all over Germany were attacked and more than ninety Jews were killed. There was so much broken glass on the streets that the attacks became known as *Kristallnacht* ("Night of the Broken Glass"). These attacks on Jews led to protests abroad. In Chicago, United States, protestors burned **swastika** flags – flags of the Nazi party. In Germany, Jews who could afford to travel to other countries hurried to do so. Over 100,000 settled in the United States between 1933 and the beginning of 1939, over 50,000 in the UK, and 3,500 in Australia.

## Building an army

Under the terms of the **Treaty of Versailles**, imposed on Germany after the First World War, Germany was only allowed an army of 100,000 men. By March 1935, however, Hitler was ready to announce a new, huge army of 500,000 men. He had slowly built his army up to this massive size, and he also wanted another half a million new recruits on top of this.

### Kristallnacht – Night of the Broken Glass

By 1938, Hitler wanted an excuse to organize a bigger attack on German Jews than anything that had taken place before. He found the excuse when Hirsch Grynszpan, a Jew living in Paris, shot a German official at the German Embassy on 6 November. Grynszpan was angry at the mistreatment of his father who had been expelled from Germany a few weeks before. When the official died from his wounds, Hitler gave orders for a night of terror across Germany. After *Kristallnacht*, German Jews were made to pay for the cost of the damage caused.

This smashed shop window was just one of the hundreds of Jewish businesses vandalised during *Kristallnacht*, 9 November 1938.

# The Berlin Olympic Games

Adolf Hitler declares the *Olympiad* (Olympic Stadium) officially open, 7 August 1936.

At the 1932 Los Angeles Olympic Games, where Germany had not been as successful as they had hoped, black athletes had achieved much success. When the Games took place in Berlin four years later, Hitler wanted to show the world what Nazi Germany could achieve in terms of sport. Nazism was built on racist ideas about the superiority of the white race (especially the German race) and the inferiority of other races. Jews and black people were regarded as inferior races. So, too, were Slavs – the racial group in large parts of the USSR.

## Sport as propaganda

From 1933, Jews were banned from sport and athletic clubs in Germany, so a **boycott** of the Berlin Games was organized in the United States. This idea was dropped when the Nazis assured the world that everyone, including Jews, could take part. Hitler knew well that a successful Olympic Games would be tremendous **propaganda** for Nazi Germany and he wanted to make sure they were successful.

Signs forbidding entry for Jews were removed from the Olympic areas and other sites where tourists were likely to visit. A US journalist who wrote for *The Nation* was fooled by these measures into thinking that Nazi Germany treated everyone the same. In August 1936, he wrote how no one could see Jews being mistreated and how everyone behaved very politely.

A short while before the Olympics began, the German boxer Max Schmeling defeated African-American Joe Louis for the world heavyweight boxing championship. Schmeling, who had a Jewish manager, was not a racist, but his victory was seen in racist terms by the Nazi government. Goebbels, a high-ranking Nazi, wrote in his diary: "Schmeling fought and won for Germany. The white defeated the black and the white was a German." Hopes were high for victory in the Olympics at the expense of black athletes.

## Owens wins gold

On the first day of the Olympics, Goebbels wrote again in his diary, though this time he was not so pleased. He recorded the fact that Germany had won only one gold medal while the United States had won three, two of which were by black athletes: "White races should be ashamed," he wrote. Jesse Owens, an African American, won four track and field gold medals and equalled the world record of 10.3 seconds for the 100 metre race.

### The world's fastest human

James Cleveland Owens was born in Alabama, United States, but moved to Ohio at the age of eight. His talent for running was spotted at school and encouraged by teachers. Universities were keen to recruit him because of his talent and he attended Ohio State University. As an African American he had to live apart from the white students, and suffered **discrimination** in many other ways. When travelling as part of the university's athletics team he had to eat and sleep separately and he was not awarded a scholarship. Even after the Berlin Olympics, having won four gold medals for his country, he was denied financial support or sponsorship because he was black.

American athlete Jesse Owens runs at the 1936 Olympic Games in Berlin.

# Living under Nazism

The Nazi government got rid of **trade unions** because they attracted many **socialists** and **communists**. Nazism was completely opposed to **communism**, and many people supported Hitler for this reason alone. At this time, anti-communists in other countries, such as Henry Ford in the United States for example, supported Hitler because of this.

A special police force, the Gestapo, was set up to deal with anyone who showed signs of not fully supporting Nazism. By 1935, 1.3 million Germans had been imprisoned for political crimes at one time or another. Many others decided to keep their heads down and say nothing.

**Anti-Semitism** – hatred of Jews – was common in Europe at the time and many Germans simply put up with the way Jews were being treated. Nazi propaganda was also important in persuading people to support Hitler. German newspapers and school textbooks encouraged anti-Semitism by showing Jews as greedy **capitalists** who could not be trusted.

*The Protocols of the Elders of Zion*, first published in 1905, was a fake document made by the Russian secret police. It claimed that there was a Jewish plot to take over the world. Hitler's anti-Semitic views were greatly influenced by this fake.

## The power of propaganda

The Nazis used the technology of the 1930s to persuade people that Hitler's government was acting in the best interest of most Germans. In an age without television, the spoken word was a powerful weapon. As well as radio broadcasts there were large Nazi gatherings where microphones could broadcast words to thousands of people. Hitler privately practised parts of his speeches in front of a mirror in order to make himself more convincing as a public speaker. Meetings would be held at night, so that huge spotlights could point towards the night sky and create a sense of drama.

Cinema was also used as a way of spreading propaganda. Goebbels ordered that a film be made of the Berlin Olympics. Leni Riefenstahl, an actress who showed a talent for film-making, was put in charge and made the film *Olympia*. Riefenstahl had also made *Triumph of the Will* in 1934, to show a Nazi Party gathering at Nuremberg, a city in Germany. This film showed Hitler descending through the crowds in an aircraft in bright sunshine. Powerful music, dramatic camera angles, and lighting were used to show Hitler as a godlike figure. Riefenstahl's work is still admired for the way it used film as propaganda, although she was accused of promoting Nazism. Riefenstahl, who died in 2003, claimed she never supported Nazi ideas.

## Listening to Hitler

A British woman witnessed Hitler speaking at Nuremberg before the war began:

"The crowd was silent, but the drums continued their steady beat. Hitler's voice boomed into the night and every now and then the crowd broke into a roar of cheers. Some of the audience began swaying back and forth, chanting 'Sieg Heil' ['Hail Victory'] over and over again. I looked at the faces around me and saw tears streaming down people's cheeks. The drums had grown louder and I suddenly felt frightened. As soon as Hitler stopped speaking the spell seemed to break and the magic vanished. His small figure suddenly became drab and unimpressive. You had to pinch yourself to realize that this was the man on whom the eyes of the world were riveted; that he alone held the lightning in his hands."

(FROM *LOOKING FOR TROUBLE* BY VIRGINIA COWLES)

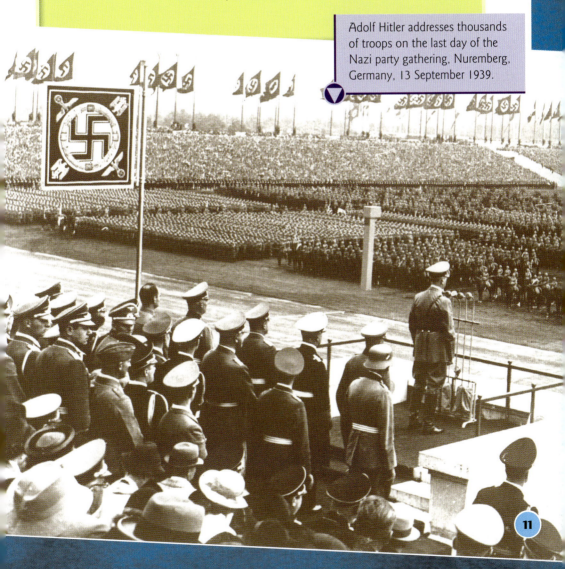

Adolf Hitler addresses thousands of troops on the last day of the Nazi party gathering, Nuremberg, Germany, 13 September 1939.

# Getting a kick out of life

The effects of the **Great Depression**, when the world **economy** went into a steep decline, were still being felt around the world in the late 1930s. In the United States, there were still over 8 million unemployed people. Poor farmers in the South and Midwest of the United States continued to **migrate** to California and industrial cities such as Detroit. In the UK, working-class families in the industrial regions were still living a hard life. Across Europe and the United States, however, people with secure jobs and a regular income were able to enjoy some of the benefits of new technology.

## Style machines

The Model T Ford had been the most successful family car for decades, and the basic design and black colour had remained unchanged. In the 1930s, Ford began to be challenged. Engineers realized that the wind resistance of vehicles was reduced if straight lines were smoothed out. This idea, called **streamlining**, enabled cars to move faster and look more attractive. The Chrysler Airflow, with a slanted windscreen and curved radiator, went on sale from 1934. As its name suggests, it was one of the first cars to benefit from the idea of a streamlined design. By 1940, the Greyhound bus, the most affordable means of public transport across the United States for people without cars, was redesigned to give it a more streamlined and stylish appearance. Shiny chrome was used to make machines look desirable.

This advertisement from the 1930s pictures the Chrysler Airflow car.

## Trendy trains and plywood

It was not only the design of cars that was influenced by ideas of streamlining. Trains also began to lose their chunky, solid appearance as the engines were redesigned to look like sleek, rocket-like machines. They were fast, too. In 1938, a UK locomotive, the Mallard, set a new world record for steam power when it reached a speed of over 125 miles (200 kilometres) per hour. Steam trains, though, were on their way out, as new trains began running on diesel.

New ideas were also affecting interior designers. Plywood was made by sticking together thin sheets of wood. It proved to be a strong and flexible material for making furniture. It was shaped and bent by steam into stylish designs.

Alvar Aalto used flexible, bendy wood in his designs, such as this one called *Armchair "41,"* from 1932.

### "I Get a Kick Out of You"

Cole Porter wrote songs in the 1930s that captured people's imaginations and became big hits. One of these songs was "I Get a Kick Out of You":

I get no kick from champagne;
Mere alcohol doesn't thrill me at all.
So tell me why should it be true
That I get a kick out of you

I get no kick in a plane
Flying too high with some guy in the sky
Is my idea of nothing to do,
Yet I get a kick out of you.

(FROM "I GET A KICK OUT OF YOU" BY COLE PORTER)

# WAR IN SPAIN AND CHINA

There was a royal scandal in the UK in 1936. Edward VIII became king in January, but in December he resigned. He wanted to marry Mrs Simpson, a divorced woman, but the Church of England would not allow this, and the king was the head of this Church. What was not well known at the time was that Edward supported the policies of Hitler. The British government knew this, and shipped him off to the Bahamas, where he became Governor, to keep him out of European politics.

## Civil war in Spain

Between 1936 and 1939, a **civil war** tore Spain apart. It came to be seen as a grisly "dress rehearsal" for the world war that would erupt in 1939. One reason for this was because innocent civilians became victims. Not only were they a deliberate target, they were also caught up in military conflicts that took place in towns and cities.

## A divided society

Spanish society was divided in a number of ways. There were rich landowners with large estates and the Catholic Church also owned a lot of the country's wealth. On the other hand, there were very poor and powerless workers in the countryside who owned little or no land. Middle-class workers in the industrial towns also had very little power. Both these groups were against the great power of the Church.

Women flee from their shattered homes in Madrid, Spain, during the Spanish Civil War, 7 December 1936.

## Causes of the war

The general division in society between right wing and left wing forces caused the war in Spain. The right wing supported the power of the Church and the landowners and did not want Spanish society to change. The left wing did want change and believed **socialism** would create a more equal society. In February 1936, elections saw the defeat of right-wing forces by a combination of left wing parties. In July the military, under General Franco, decided to attack the new government. They were worried that a left wing government would weaken the power of the landowners and the Church. Left wing groups organized resistance to General Franco and the result was a bitter civil war.

### The International Brigades

The groups fighting Franco, called the Republicans, received support from a total of 59,000 volunteers from 55 countries. They were known as the International Brigades. Several famous European and American writers that believed in the Republicans' cause, including Ernest Hemingway, went to Spain to support them.

## Social revolution

Fierce fighting developed as Franco's army set about capturing the large cities of Barcelona and Madrid. Left wing groups fought Franco and, at the same time, set about creating a **social revolution**. Peasants in the countryside were encouraged to take over the land from rich landowners and farm it together. Workers in the cities took over their places of work. Everything from shoeshining to public transport was organized and run by the workers themselves. They worked to earn a living, but, being socialists, they did not work to earn large profits. Churches were burned down and priests were murdered for supporting General Franco.

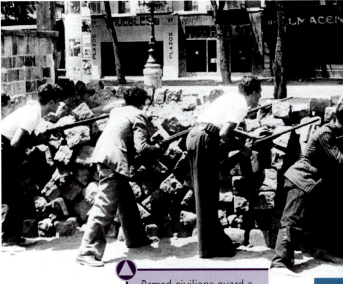

Armed civilians guard a barricade in Barcelona, Spain, around 1936.

# Guernica

General Franco and his army were supported with weapons and men from Italy and Germany. Both these countries were ruled by dictators: Hitler in Germany and Mussolini in Italy. They wanted Franco to crush the left wing forces in Spain so that socialism and communism would be weakened in Europe as a whole.

## Bombing Guernica

In April 1937, the German air force attacked the small Spanish town of Guernica. Flying in low over the defenceless town, they destroyed three-quarters of the buildings, killing 1,600 inhabitants. The Spanish artist, Pablo Picasso, expressed his outrage in a painting that became world famous. He worked in a passion and completed the huge canvas, 7.6 metres (25 feet) by 3.4 metres (11 feet) in 3 weeks.

## Picasso's painting

Franco won the Spanish Civil War with the help of Germany and Italy. The left-wing forces argued amongst themselves and this had weakened them. After 1939, when Franco had won the civil war, Picasso would not allow his painting to be exhibited in Spain. It was shipped to New York, United States, and stayed there until 1981, after the death of Franco, when it was put on display in Spain's national gallery in Madrid.

In 1940, Picasso was living in Paris, which by then was occupied by the German army. The Nazis visited his apartment and noticed a painting of Guernica on a table. The officer looked at the painting and asked, "Did you do this?" "No," replied Picasso, "You did."

## The meaning of Guernica

The German commander in charge of the attack on Guernica, von Richthofen, defended what he had done. He thought that war meant that anything could be done if it helped defeat the enemy. He argued that by attacking civilians and spreading fear, the enemy would be weakened. The same approach would later be used in the Second World War. The attack on Guernica became a symbol of the Spanish Civil War. It also became a symbol of how wars would be fought in the future.

### An eye-witness account

A priest, Father Alberto Onaindia, witnessed the attack:

"I arrived at Guernica on 26 April, at 4:40 p.m. I had hardly left the car when the bombardments began. The people were terrified. They fled, abandoning their livestock in the market place. The bombardment lasted until 7:45 p.m. ... The planes descended very low, the machine-gun fire tearing up the woods and roads, in whose gutters, huddled together, lay old men, women, and children. Before long, it was impossible to see as far as 500 yards (457 metres), owing to the heavy smoke."

(FROM A CONCISE HISTORY OF THE SPANISH CIVIL WAR BY PAUL PRESTON)

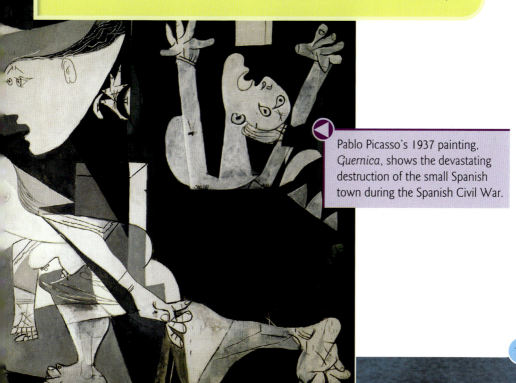

Pablo Picasso's 1937 painting, *Guernica*, shows the devastating destruction of the small Spanish town during the Spanish Civil War.

# New leaders in Japan

Over the first quarter of the 20th century, Japan set out to achieve the same kind of wealth and progress as Western countries like the United States and the UK. Modern industry and European styles of dress were introduced, and the country became an **ally** of the UK and the United States during the First World War. In 1929, the **Wall Street Crash** shattered Japan when other countries stopped buying its biggest export, silk, and millions of small farmers faced ruin. **Nationalists** blamed the West. They wanted to stop trying to be like the West and called for the building of an empire so that Japan would not have to rely on the West for **raw materials**.

## Invasion of China

As part of its empire-building, Japan invaded China in 1931, and seized the northern region called Manchuria. At first, Europe and the United States were too busy dealing with their own economic problems to get involved. At the same time, military leaders in Japan set about **assassinating** politicians and businessmen who had been involved in trade with Western countries. Japan began to turn inwards and military leaders became more influential in the country's government.

Japan wanted to extend its empire in China and began building up its armed forces. Plans were drawn up to create a wider empire, extending across Asia and the Pacific. Japan was criticised by the United States and European countries for interfering in China. But, the United States, itself, was interfering in Latin America, and European countries already had their own empires. Japan thought it had just as much right to create its own empire.

This bar chart shows how Japanese military spending rose dramatically during the 1930s.

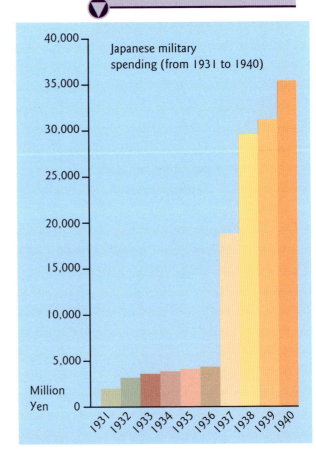

Japanese military spending (from 1931 to 1940)

Million Yen

## The rape of Nanking

In July 1937, a full-scale war against China was launched and the capital, which was then Nanking (now called Nanjing), was captured in December. There then followed a massacre of the city's inhabitants that became known as "the rape of Nanking." It is estimated that over a quarter of a million Chinese civilians died.

The United States, UK, and France did not want China to fall to the Japanese. They gave support to the Chinese who were fighting the invaders. Japan, however, depended on the United States and the British Empire for vital raw materials such as oil, rubber, and tin. The United States made it clear that it would stop exports to Japan if necessary. What would Japan do if this happened?

### Genocide in Nanking

"Tens of thousands of young men were rounded up and herded to the outer areas of the city. They were mowed down by machine guns, used for **bayonet** practice, or soaked with gasoline and burned alive. For months the streets of the city were heaped with corpses and reeked with the stench of rotting human flesh."

(FROM *THE RAPE OF NANKING:*
*THE FORGOTTEN HOLOCAUST OF*
*WORLD WAR II* BY
IRIS CHANG.)

Victorious Japanese troops roll past government buildings in Nanking on their invasion of the capital, 13 December 1937.

# THE SECOND WORLD WAR

By 1938, it was clear to many that Germany was set on war and the UK started to prepare itself for air attacks. In September 1938, the UK Prime Minister, Neville Chamberlain, travelled to Germany for his third meeting with Hitler. He returned with an agreement that he claimed would provide "peace in our time," but 38 million gas masks were being distributed across the UK. Poisonous gas, it was feared, would be used in any attack on the country.

## The road to war

In March 1936, Hitler's army reoccupied an area in western Germany, called the Rhineland, even though it was supposed to stay **demilitarized** under the terms of the Treaty of Versailles. Two years later, German forces were welcomed into Austria, which became united with Germany. In Czechoslovakia there were 3 million Germans living in a region called the Sudetenland, and in September1938, Hitler also demanded the right to rule this region.

A conference was held in Munich in September 1938, between Hitler and the leaders of the UK, French, and Italian governments. Small and powerless, the Czechoslovak government did not take part in the conference and had no say in the agreement that eventually gave Hitler the Sudetenland.

Mussolini, the dictator of Italy, attended the Munich conference as an ally of Germany. Stalin, the leader of the USSR, had been left out of the Munich talks. The USSR had earlier suggested making a **defence treaty** with the UK and France against Germany, but this idea was not taken up. In August 1939, Stalin thought he could protect the USSR from a German attack by making a deal with Hitler. They agreed to divide up Poland between them.

Young British school children take part in a gas-mask drill in preparation for German air attacks.

## Poland invaded

The UK had a treaty with Poland that said if the country were attacked, the UK would go to its defence. After the Munich meeting, Hitler felt confident that the UK would once more back down and not face up to German aggression. So, on 1 September 1939, Poland was invaded. The UK now knew that unless it stood up to Hitler, the Nazis would take over all of Europe.

German soldiers march through a Polish street after the German invasion in September 1939.

## The USSR and Nazi Germany

The deal made between the USSR and Germany in 1939 was torn apart two years later when Hitler ordered an invasion of the USSR. In 1939, however, both sides had good reasons to make a deal. Hitler wanted to invade Poland without the risk of being attacked by the USSR. Stalin wanted to protect the USSR from the risk of being invaded by Germany. He also wanted to buy some time to build up the **Soviet** Army. Once Poland was defeated, however, and most of western Europe conquered, Hitler was ready to invade the USSR and destroy communism.

# War in Europe

After Poland had been invaded, the UK and then France declared war on Germany. Australia, New Zealand, and Canada, allies of the UK, and members of the British Empire and **Commonwealth**, soon followed. Australian troops were first shipped to England in November 1939. Countries opposing Germany became known as the **Allies**. Countries supporting Germany became known as the **Axis powers**. India joined the Allies and produced the world's largest volunteer army with over 2.5 million men.

## Axis victories

German forces quickly overran Poland and the country was forced to surrender before the end of September. UK troops and equipment arrived in France and waited for the German advance, which did not finally get started until May 1940. The attack was slow in coming – a US journalist described the early months of inactivity as the "phoney war" – but when it came it was impossible to stop. Winston Churchill, who became the new UK Prime Minister in 1940, had to struggle with the speed of Axis victories. In only six weeks, Germany conquered Norway, the Netherlands, Belgium, Luxembourg, and then France.

This map of western Europe, shows the extent of Nazi domination by June 1940.

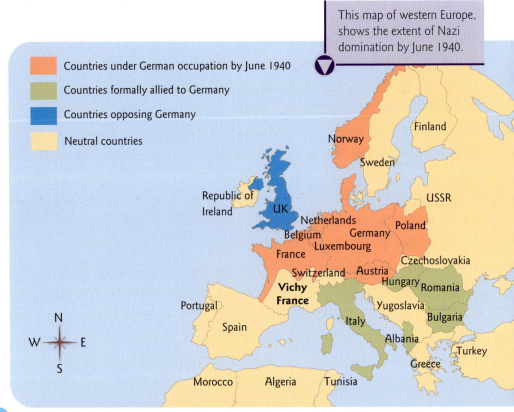

Countries under German occupation by June 1940

Countries formally allied to Germany

Countries opposing Germany

Neutral countries

Finland

Norway

Sweden

Republic of Ireland

UK

USSR

Netherlands

Belgium Germany Poland

Luxembourg

France

Czechoslovakia

Switzerland Austria

Hungary Romania

**Vichy France**

Portugal

Yugoslavia

Bulgaria

Spain

Italy

Albania

Turkey

Greece

N

W  E

S

Morocco Algeria Tunisia

## Dunkirk

German forces were better organized and better trained than their enemies and western Europe struggled under their superior strength. UK forces were pushed back towards Dunkirk, on the northern coast of France, and plans for an **evacuation** got under way. Around 370,000 troops were shipped back to the UK, 139,000 of them French, but all their equipment had to be left behind.

## Battle of Britain

Hitler laid plans for an invasion of the UK, and the Nazi air force commander, Hermann Göring, promised to defeat the British Royal Air Force (RAF) in a couple of weeks. This was meant to prepare the way for an easy invasion, but Göring's campaign failed. The fight between the German air force, the *Luftwaffe*, and the RAF took place in the skies over southern England between July and September 1940. This became known as the Battle of Britain. The lack of an outright victory persuaded Hitler to postpone an invasion, and he concentrated instead on an invasion of the USSR. Once the USSR was defeated, conquering the UK would be a simple matter.

## Battle of the Atlantic

German submarines, called U-boats, tried to sink **merchant ships** taking vital supplies of oil and food to the UK from the United States. This became known as the Battle of the Atlantic. Roosevelt was re-elected President of the United States in 1940, and he allowed the United States to lend supplies to the UK in return for a promise of payment after the war. At this stage, though, most Americans did not think their country would get involved in the war. It was a European war, one that did not seem to affect US interests.

## Evacuation

In Britain, families in cities could send their children away to live in the countryside where there was less risk of being killed in bombing raids. Wealthy families with large homes opened their doors to nearly 2 million children from the cities within the first few weeks of war. Although some children settled happily, many others were very homesick and drifted back to their families in the city during the war.

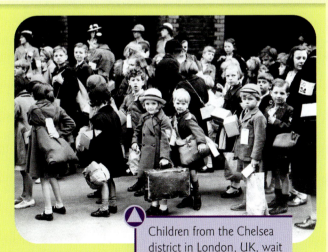

Children from the Chelsea district in London, UK, wait to be evacuated to the countryside, 31 August 1939.

# The United States join the war

## America's attitude

Hitler invaded the USSR in the summer of 1941 and this worried the US government. If the USSR were conquered, the Nazi empire would stretch from western Europe to the east of the USSR in Asia. It would be powerful enough to challenge the United States. President Roosevelt supported the UK as much as possible, but US public opinion was strongly against the idea of military involvement in the European war.

Japan was also causing alarm. It was seeking to expand its power. The United States did not intend to let Japan challenge United States interests in China, or take control of the Pacific.

## Japan's attitude

Japanese leaders knew that the United States was opposed to its expansion. The United States was providing loans to China to help support its war of resistance against Japan. In July 1940, the United States stopped selling aviation fuel to Japan, as well as some types of iron and steel.

Japan needed oil that came from central Indonesia, part of the empire of the Netherlands. The Dutch government, which had turned to the UK after Hitler's occupation of the Netherlands, refused to sell it. By the summer of 1941, Japan decided to attack the United States.

In the second half of 1941, tension mounted. All sales of US oil to Japan were stopped. The Japanese economy was in danger of collapsing and a decision was made to attack and destroy the US fleet at Pearl Harbor in Hawaii. At the same time, Japan would invade the European **colonies** in South-East Asia and seize their **natural resources**. Japan would be strengthened and, without a navy, the United States would have to make a deal and accept the new Japanese empire.

### Leonard J. Fox remembers

Leonard J. Fox was on the USS *Helena* when he saw bombs raining down from planes in the sky:

"Within the next few moments all hell broke loose. Torpedo planes swooped in from almost over my head. First the *Oklahoma* was hit, then it was the *West Virginia* taking blows. Now, as I looked on unbelievingly, the *California* erupted, and then the *Arizona*. Everywhere there were men swimming for their lives in the fire-covered waters of Pearl Harbor."

(FROM *THE PACIFIC CAMPAIGN* BY DAN VAN DER VAT)

# Pearl Harbor

On 7 December 1941, the Japanese launched a surprise attack on the US fleet at Pearl Harbor. The Americans were not expecting Japanese aircraft carriers, supported by oil tankers for refuelling, to secretly sail to within 199 miles (320 kilometres) of Hawaii. From there, Japanese bombers took off and headed for Hawaii. Around 180 planes swooped low over the naval base in 2 attacks lasting 2 hours. They sank or crippled 21 US ships and more than 2,500 servicemen died in the attack.

The USS *California* burns in Pearl Harbor after the Japanese attack on 7 December 1941.

With the German invasion of the USSR, the threat of a Nazi invasion of the UK became less likely. People in the UK were encouraged to grow their own vegetables, as a way of dealing with food shortages, and "Dig for Victory" became a popular slogan. A government notice went up in hotel bathrooms requesting that, "As part of your personal share in the Battle for Fuel you are asked NOT to exceed five inches of water in this bath." There was a strong sense of **solidarity** as people realized they had to work together if they were going to survive.

## The war spreads

In June 1940, Italy joined the war on Hitler's side. The UK wanted to protect the Mediterranean as part of the sea route to its empire in Asia. This led to UK, Australian, and Indian troops fighting Italian forces that were stationed in Libya in North Africa. German forces then arrived in North Africa to help the Italians. By 1942, the war had spread to the Middle East, and the UK fought in Iraq to remove the government, which supported Hitler. Far more important than these battlefields, however, was the German invasion of the USSR in June 1941.

# War in the USSR

Hitler's ambition to conquer the USSR was stopped by fierce resistance from the people whose land he was invading, and by the harsh Russian winter. The German advance, which had begun as a huge success, was halted outside Moscow before the end of 1941. With 3 million of his enemy dead in the USSR and another 3 million captured, Hitler set about completing the conquest of the USSR in 1942. The plan was to capture the industrial complex around the city of Stalingrad and from there, capture the oil fields of the Caucasus region. Then German troops would move north to seize Moscow.

A year later, in November 1942, the Germans at Stalingrad received a deadly shock. A USSR **Red Army** of over a million men attacked the Germans and surrounded them. It was one of the fiercest battles in the whole war, but the **Soviet** soldiers finally gained an advantage. The German army surrendered and Hitler was furious.

British soldiers trek across the North African desert in shorts as the battlefield extends into very different and hostile climates, around 1943.

## The Russian winter

Heinrich Haape in the German army began to realize what a winter war in the USSR would be like:

"I stopped to think of the armies marching on Moscow across open country at this very moment. All that those men had received so far were their woollen Kopfschutzer [hats]; the winter clothing had still not arrived. What was happening to those poor men's feet (as I knew the ordinary army boot retained very little warmth)?

At that time the thermometer showed only twelve degrees below zero. Temperatures would drop to minus twenty-four degrees, minus thirty-six degrees, minus forty-eight degrees – perhaps even lower. It was beyond thinking – a temperature four times colder than a deep freezer."

(FROM *MOSCOW TRAM STOP* BY HEINRICH HAAPE)

# War in the Pacific

When Pearl Harbor was attacked, three US aircraft carriers based at Hawaii happened to be out at sea. The importance of this was not obvious at first, especially as the Japanese were very successful in their other attacks on the **Allies** in Asia. What mattered, though, was that the US fleet had not been entirely wiped out. The United States was still able to fight at sea.

## The Philippines

The Philippines was a major military base for the United States in Asia. There, under the command of General MacArthur, were 30,000 US troops, 100,000 Philippine soldiers, a large number of bombers, and over 100 fighter aircraft. Just 9 hours after news of Pearl Harbor first reached the base, the Japanese attacked from the air and destroyed half the aircraft.

At the same time, Japanese troops landed on the Philippine islands of Luzon and Mindanao, with the intention of trapping the enemy. MacArthur withdrew troops to a narrow strip of land called the Bataan peninsula. The Japanese attacked. MacArthur himself was ordered to withdraw from Bataan to Australia.

In April 1942, the Allied forces under siege surrendered to the Japanese. Nearly 80,000 survivors were forced to march 65 miles (105 kilometres) to a prison camp and the trek became known as the Bataan Death March. Some 5,000–10,000 Philippinos and over 600 Americans lost their lives along the way due to starvation, exhaustion, and brutal mistreatment.

## Japanese victories

Japanese troops landed in Malaysia, 2 hours before the first planes were reaching Pearl Harbor. The Japanese troops were well organized and very efficient. They pushed the British-led troops, mostly Indians and some Australians, south towards the UK base at Singapore, which surrendered in February 1942. By April 1942, the greater part of the Dutch East Indies (Indonesia) was under Japanese control.

Hitler knew the United States was supporting the UK and after Pearl Harbor he declared war on the United States. He thought they were already beaten.

## Sea battles

The Battle of the Coral Sea in May 1942, between US and Japanese warships, was the first battle in history in which the opposing sides never saw one another. They relied on aircraft to find and attack one another's ships. Neither side won an outright victory, but it stopped Australia from being cut off and open to invasion.

The Japanese intended to complete the destruction of the US fleet at the Battle of Midway in June 1942. Their plan was to lure the US fleet to Midway Island and destroy it from the air and by sea. The United States, however, had cracked Japanese secret coded messages and, planning their own surprise, defeated their enemy.

## Navajo code

The enemy could pick up radio, so a code that could not easily be broken was of great value. A United States engineer, who had grown up on Navajo reservations, suggested using the Native American language as a code for sending and receiving radio messages. The enemy would not understand the language and Navajo speakers were very willing to help. Some military terms had no equivalent Navajo word, but this problem was solved using suitable words from the natural world:

fish = ship       bird = plane          whale = battleship       shark = destroyer
hummingbird = fighter plane      eggs = bombs

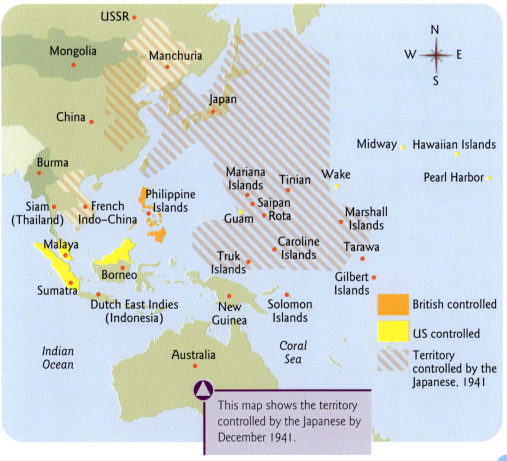

This map shows the territory controlled by the Japanese by December 1941.

# Fighting back

The island of Guadalcanal became a battlefield for control of the south Pacific after US troops landed there in August 1942. Land battles on the island were accompanied by several battles out at sea near Guadalcanal. The United States was only able to force the Japanese to start withdrawing their troops from the island in early 1943.

## Fighting for islands

MacArthur led Australian troops from the south side of New Guinea to encounter Japanese troops on the north side. The single route across the mountains, the Kokoda trail, became a desperate battleground as soldiers on both sides struggled to survive in the jungle. Fighting lasted through the second half of 1942 and thousands died.

Early in 1943, the United States was ready to try and force the Japanese off other Pacific islands, and in the course of the year fierce battles took place on New Georgia, Tarawa, and other islands.

By early 1944, the United States was ready to take the Mariana Islands – Saipan, Tinian, Rota, and Guam – and the last island was captured in August. The Japanese tried to stop the landings and gathered nine aircraft carriers for what became the battle of the Philippine Sea in June. They were not successful and the way was open for MacArthur to set about recapturing the Philippines.

US Navy bombers return from a bombing run on Japanese airfields at Param Island (now part of the Federated States of Micronesia) February 1944.

## Germany in trouble

After he had failed to capture Stalingrad, Hitler prepared for a final battle with the USSR. It took place near the city of Kursk in eastern Europe. The Soviet general, Zhukov, was ready for the battle and his well-organized forces broke the German lines. Hitler's army was now in retreat and Zhukov was able to advance westwards. The Soviets had broken the Nazis, though with a tremendous loss of life.

## Making plans

In January 1943, with Stalin busy dealing with the German invaders, Roosevelt and Churchill met in North Africa to discuss plans. Roosevelt was keen to push forward with plans to land in German-occupied northern France, while Churchill was interested in the Mediterranean region. It was agreed that an Anglo-American invasion of southern Italy would take place in 1943, with plans for a large-scale invasion of France in 1944.

### "Any gum, chum?"

A friendly invasion of the UK took place in 1943 and 1944 as Americans, Australians, and Canadians arrived in preparation for the coming landings in France. For many in the UK the African-American servicemen were the first black people they had seen. They did not know that racist attitudes meant that no African-American soldier could have a higher rank than a white soldier in the same unit. Nor was it known that the authorities in the UK and Australia had objected to black soldiers being stationed in their countries. One thing that was noticed was that US soldiers had chewing gum, which was not readily available in Britain, and children pestered them for it. "Any gum, chum?" became a national catchphrase.

An African-American soldier dances with a British Women's Auxiliary Air Force member at Paramount Dance Hall, England, 1944.

# CIVILIANS AT WAR

Civilian life in the UK was transformed by the war. Children were **evacuated**, women did jobs previously thought suitable only for men, and food was **rationed**. Big cities such as London, Coventry, Liverpool, and Belfast were heavily bombed. In Australia, Darwin was bombed 64 times between 1942 and 1943. In London, to stay safe from the bombing, citizens took to sleeping in the underground train stations. Art treasures from museums and galleries were also stored there.

## "The final solution"

Early in the war, Jews were collected together and forced to live in certain areas of German-occupied cities, called **ghettoes**. Here, without employment and food, thousands were left to die. Then, in January 1942, a meeting took place outside Berlin, at Wannsee, attended by high-ranking Nazis. The decision was made to organize the killing of all the Jews in Europe. They called it "the final solution". The plan was very nearly successful and by the end of the war only about 300,000 Jews survived in Europe. Around 6 million were murdered in what has become known as the Holocaust.

## Organized mass murder

Nazism believed that the German race was a superior race and that it should be kept pure. This meant the mass murder of other types of people. Any group regarded as imperfect by the Nazis was to be exterminated. This meant the organized killing of the physically and mentally handicapped, homosexuals, and Gypsies – anyone, in fact, that was not part of the "pure" German race.

The grim entrance to the German concentration camp of Auschwitz, constructed in Poland in 1942.

The Nazis also wanted to destroy communists because communism was also seen as a threat to the idea of a superior German race. The Slav people of the USSR were, like the Jews, regarded as an inferior race that should be exterminated or enslaved. Following the invasion of the USSR, hundreds of thousands of communists and Slavs were killed. Killing large numbers of people one-by-one began to take too much time and effort. So extermination camps were set up – where people were killed on a large scale.

## Death camps and work camps

In Poland six **death camps** were built. Their names were Auschwitz, Belzec, Chelmno, Majdanek, Sobibor, and Treblinka. Jews from all over Europe were transported by train to these camps and murdered by poisonous gas. Bodies were cremated after gassing, and their hair, glasses, shoes, and gold fillings were collected because money could be earned from these materials. The young and the able became slaves and were worked to death in **concentration camps**. Auschwitz, the largest death camp, had several concentration camps nearby.

### Uncomfortable facts

1. The Allies knew about the Holocaust but neither the United States nor the UK did anything to try and stop it. One explanation is that their priority was to defeat their enemies. It is an uncomfortable fact that some action, such as bombing the railway line to Auschwitz, or the camp itself, could have been taken but was not.
2. The Catholic Church, aware of what was happening, did not publicly condemn the Nazis or speak out against the rounding up of 8,000 Jews in Rome in 1943.

Starved prisoners stand motionless in a concentration camp in Ebensee, Austria, on the day Allied forces liberated the camp, 7 May 1945.

# The suffering of civilians

Unlike most previous wars, the Second World War was not just happening on battlefields in foreign countries. It was fought in cities and villages. Civilians were killed in millions; women and even children joined the fighting. Of all those killed during the war, three-quarters of them were civilians.

## The siege of Leningrad

The city of Leningrad (now St Petersburg) was besieged for 890 days when the USSR was invaded in 1941. Rationing meant a tiny daily allowance of only 125 grams (4.4 ounces) of bread and people died of starvation as well as the winter cold. Conditions were so desperate that **cannibalism** occurred – 300 people were executed for this crime. By the time winter came to an end in 1942, 650,000 civilians had died. When the siege finally ended in January 1944, about 600,000 people were left in a city that had had a population of 2.8 million in 1941.

Two stunned women sit in the ruins of destroyed buildings after the German bombardment of Leningrad, Russia, 1942.

## Civilians in Asia

The war between Japan and China resulted in Chinese civilians living elsewhere in Asia, being murdered or mistreated, in countries under Japanese occupation. In Singapore, for example, many thousands were driven to beaches and machine-gunned by Japanese soldiers. Pacific islanders were forced to work and fight for the armies of both the Japanese and the Allies and sometimes ended up killing one another.

Japanese conquests meant that hundreds of thousands of European civilians, living in what had been colonies, were treated harshly by the Japanese and most were imprisoned. Many did not survive the lack of food and medical facilities. The Japanese used 300,000 Asian civilians for slave labour, along with prisoners of war, in the building of a railway line from Thailand to Burma. They suffered terribly, with one in three civilians dying, while one in five of the prisoners of war died.

## The cost of Resistance

Civilians in Nazi-occupied Europe suffered terribly from food shortages and thousands died because of this. Attempts to resist and fight Nazi control were often met by heavy punishment and in Greece whole villages were massacred in acts of revenge. In 1944, when an uprising failed in Warsaw, Poland, the German response was savage and 200,000 civilians lost their lives.

### Japanese-Americans

After the attack on Pearl Harbor, all Japanese people living in California, Oregon, and Washington in the United States, were thought of as possible spies. In February 1942, Roosevelt signed an order that moved nearly 120,000 of them into isolated camps behind barbed-wire fences. Two-thirds of them were US citizens and many were under the age of 21. They were forced to live in these camps for the next two to three years and conditions were often harsh. In December 1942, protests in one camp led to the military police being called in and two people died after being shot.

A Japanese-American man addresses fellow prisoners at a detention camp in Puyallop, Washington, United States, 9 August 1942.

# Bombing civilians

## The Blitz

In September 1940, Germany began bombing UK cities. This continued until mid May 1941. Many bombs missed their military or commercial targets and more than 40,000 civilians were killed in the winter of 1940–1941. It was called the Blitz in the UK, after the German *Blitzkrieg* (meaning "lightning war"), but the country survived with the help of vital supplies from the United States. Towards the end of the war, German scientists developed the V-2 – a rocket bomb that cruised towards its target without a sound. Around 500 of them landed in London, killing 9,000 citizens.

## Bombing Germany

The UK fought back against Germany with a bombing campaign that deliberately targeted civilian areas of cities, leading to half a million deaths. The intention was to **demoralize** the enemy and, it was hoped, shorten the war. This did not work. If anything, the bombing drew German citizens together against the UK. But, despite this resolve, by February 1945, Germany was nearly beaten. UK and US forces decided to make a final attack and bomb the city of Dresden. An estimated 70,000–80,000 people died in one night in the bombing.

## Bombing Asians

Pacific Islanders were not treated very well, either by the Japanese or the Allies. Tens of thousands of New Guineans, for example, died as a result of island bombing. The civilian population of Japanese cities suffered terribly as a result of bombing and a quarter of a million people died. Unlike UK and German cities, there were no sheltering places where they could find protection from the bombing and Tokyo suffered badly from fires caused by bombs. In one, on 9 March 1945, 83,000 civilians died. In August of the same year, even more civilians were to die when **atom bombs** were dropped on the cities of Hiroshima and Nagasaki.

Female workers remove debris from the shell of the *Hofkirche*, the Catholic Cathedral in Dresden, Germany, after the Allied bombing attack, February 1945.

## Dogs in war

In most countries that were being bombed, a noisy siren warned people that enemy aircraft were approaching. When the danger had passed, a different "All Clear" siren was usually heard.

"There is evidence that dogs and cats soon learned to recognize the sound of the siren. Some even claimed they could distinguish between the warning and the All Clear. Some animals began to move even before the siren. Dogs, with their well-developed hearing, sometimes picked up the noise of distant gunfire or aircraft before human ears could do so."

(FROM *HOW WE LIVED THEN* BY NORMAN LONGMATE)

The Soviets used "mine dogs" to attack German tanks. The dogs, laden with explosives and a detonator sticking up from their backs, were trained to crawl under enemy tanks. However, the dogs were trained using Soviet tanks, and often ran at these and not the enemy tanks. Several Soviet tanks were destroyed in this way. Some Soviet tank crews prevented this from happening by shooting mine dogs that ran at their tanks. Many dogs who accidentally strayed near the battlefields on the Eastern front were also shot.

An Alsatian dog awaits orders from his Soviet soldier-owner, around 1940.

# The women's war

Women were involved in the Second World War at all levels, including combat. The Soviet army included over 250,000 women by 1945 and they fought as machine-gunners and snipers, as well as soldiers. The Soviet 46th Guards Women's Night Light-Bomber Regiment flew in biplanes that were serviced by female mechanics.

## Rosie the Riveter

As more and more men were called up to join the armed forces, their peacetime jobs needed to be filled by women. Suddenly, women were successfully doing jobs that had been considered suitable only for men. In the United States 8 million women found jobs, and in the shipbuilding industry the number of female employees rose from 16 in 1941 to 160,000 in 1943. Propaganda films were made to encourage women to no longer think of themselves just as housewives. The most memorable of these films, *Rosie the Riveter*, featured a real person who went to work at an aircraft factory in Detroit. Rose Will Monroe, the star of the film, had wanted to train as a pilot to fly transport missions during the war but she was turned down because of being a woman.

One of the female machinists, who inspired the film *Rosie the Riveter*, working in a United States arms manufacturing plant, around 1943.

## Baby riots

In the UK, the shortage of workers was so severe that women were **conscripted**. This meant they were forced by law to do "national service." Many women had to take up employment in many types of work.

Many UK women worked in what became known as the Land Army, growing food. This helped against the Axis powers that were trying to starve the UK into surrender by cutting off its imports. The problem for many women employed in war work was the lack of nurseries for their young children. In 1941, women protestors, marching with prams and with placards demanding better childcare facilities, produced headlines about "baby riots" in newspapers.

## Prisoners of war

It was not only captured soldiers who ended up in prisoner of war camps. When Japan invaded the Dutch colonies, and **territory** in Asia that had been UK colonies, thousands of women and children were captured and treated as prisoners of war. Asian women and children were sent to work and died building the Thailand-Burma railway line.

### Women in combat

This account describes a Soviet tank being attacked by German forces in the USSR:

"A second direct hit brought it to a standstill, but in spite of its hopeless position it defended itself while a tank-killer team advanced on it. Finally it burst into flame and only then did the turret open. A woman in tanker uniform climbed out. She was the wife and co-fighter of a tank company commander who, killed by the first hit, lay beside her in the turret."

(FROM TANK BY PATRICK WRIGHT)

Soviet military forces included over 250,000 women in the Second World War, such as the woman pictured here on a Soviet battleship.

# VICTORY IN SIGHT

By 1944, the war had turned in favour of the Allies. For the UK, United States, and Commonwealth soldiers in the UK, however, an important battle was yet to come. It was agreed that Allied troops would have to land in Europe and fight to force Hitler into surrender. In April 1944, while practising for the landings, 749 US soldiers and sailors died after 3 ships were ambushed by German torpedo boats off the Devon coast. This was kept secret for 50 days in case news of the disaster lowered morale or tipped off the Germans.

## Victories in the Pacific

The Japanese knew they had to stop the United States retaking the Philippines in late 1944. Defeat would allow the United States to advance towards Japan. What took place, the Battle of Leyte Gulf, was the largest naval battle in world history. For the first time, *kamikaze* pilots deliberately crashed their planes on to a US ship and sank it. The Japanese, though, still lost the battle.

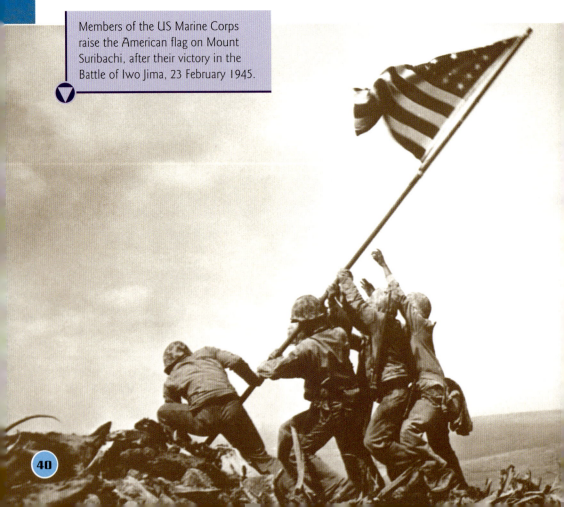

Members of the US Marine Corps raise the American flag on Mount Suribachi, after their victory in the Battle of Iwo Jima, 23 February 1945.

In February 1945, over 100,000 US soldiers landed on Iwo Jima, just over 621 miles (1,000 kilometres) south of Tokyo. Resistance by the Japanese was fierce. Final victory by the United States was caught in the famous photograph of the US flag being raised on the island. The human cost was terrible: over 1 in 3 US marines were killed, nearly 4,000 in total, and over 20,000 Japanese lost their lives – all for an island only 5 miles (8 kilometres) long.

After Iwo Jima, the island of Okinawa was captured and from there an invasion of mainland Japan would be possible. The United States was reluctant, however, to invade Japan as so many peope had already been killed.

## Preparing for D-Day

While islands in the Pacific were being bitterly fought over in the first half of 1944, a very important secret was being kept in southern England. Everyone, including Hitler, knew that the Allies would try to land in northern France, but where exactly the landings would take place was a carefully kept secret.

### "This is it my darling, I have to go"

David Holdsworth, who was suddenly ordered to move to a camp in preparation for the invasion, says farewell to his wife. Even at this stage, he did not know where he would be landing:

"David kissed me. 'This is it my darling, I have to go.' He went quietly and quickly down the stairs, the front door banged. I looked out of the window and watched them [David and his brother] ride off together on the swaying motorbike into the night. The next ten days seemed like an eternity. Suddenly one night the sky was full of aircraft and I knew the invasion had begun. It was almost a relief."

(FROM VICTORY IN EUROPE, JULIAN THOMPSON)

# D-Day in Europe

The secret plan of the Allies was to land US, UK, and Commonwealth troops on the beaches of Normandy in northern France. The Germans were tricked into thinking that the Allies would land at the port of Calais. The Allies pretended to be gathering troops and ships on the UK coast opposite Calais and built fake army camps to trick the Germans. The plan was successful, and on invasion day – 6 June 1944 (which became known as D-Day) – half the German forces were stationed around Calais for the expected invasion.

Within days of D-Day, as agreed between the leaders of the United States, the USSR, and the UK, the Soviets mounted a surprise attack on the Germans in eastern Europe. It was successful and allowed the Soviets to move westwards through Bulgaria. By January 1945, the USSR army set its sights on Berlin.

Troops climb off a landing barge on to the beach of Normandy, France, during the Allied invasion on D-Day, 6 June 1944.

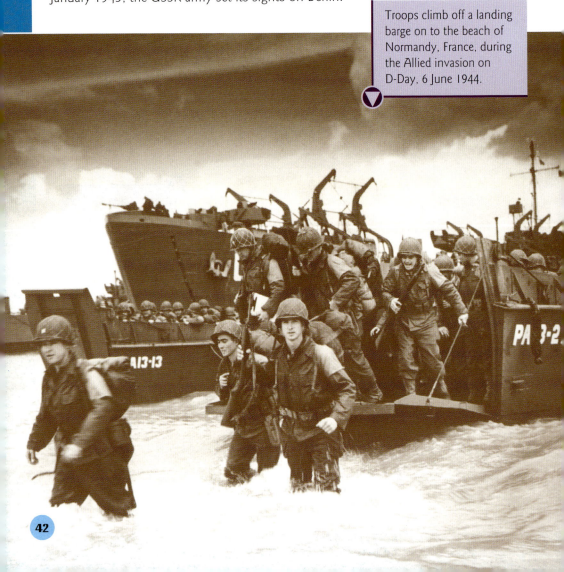

By the end of D-Day, around a hundred and fifty thousand soldiers had landed on the five code-named beaches of Normandy. The months of careful organization had paid off because the operation was largely successful. On Omaha beach, however, more than 1,000 men died and it took most of the day to take control. The commander considered calling off the landing and diverting the troops to one of the other beaches. It was a struggle but, in the end, a breakthrough was made.

Despite the success of D-Day, the Allies still had to defeat the Germans and this was no easy task. German soldiers waiting for them in France had more experience of fighting and had better tanks and rifles. By September, though, with about 2 million Allied troops in France, the Allies had almost reached the borders of Germany. There was one last counter-attack, which took the Allies by surprise, known as the Battle of the Bulge. But this failed and it was only a matter of time before the war in Europe ended.

## "Poles apart"

Dwight D. Eisenhower was the US general in overall charge of the D-Day operation. He was popularly known as Ike and grew up in Kansas, United States. His family were not wealthy, but Eisenhower successfully worked his way up through the army without ever actually experiencing a war. He had a talent for organization and for getting people to work together. His popularity after the war helped to make him the US President between 1953 and 1961.

General Dwight D. Eisenhower in a 1945 photo.

Bernard Law Montgomery, popularly known as Monty, was the UK general. Compared to Eisenhower, he had a privileged background. He went to a private school and trained at England's top military academy at Sandhurst. Many people found him stubborn and arrogant, but he understood the soldier's life and won respect because of this. Montgomery himself said that "Ike and I were poles apart" and they did not like each other.

Sir Bernard Law Montgomery, Chief of Imperial General Staff of the UK, during the Second World War.

As Eisenhower was in overall command, Montgomery was promoted to the British rank of Field Marshal to compensate for not being in complete charge. The US army had no high-ranking position that was equal to this, so a new rank was invented for Eisenhower – a five-star general.

# THE END OF THE SECOND WORLD WAR

Germany surrendered on 7 May 1945. Once the news reached the UK, VE (Victory in Europe) Day was announced on 8 May and celebrations were held. London witnessed the largest celebrations with hundreds of laughing girls and US sailors forming a conga line down the middle of Piccadilly. The war in Asia, however, had not ended and bitter fighting continued there.

## Europeans on the move

All across Europe, millions of people went on the move as they found out the Nazis had been beaten. Over half a million Germans were expelled from Hungary, Yugoslavia, and Romania, and 2.5 million from Czechoslovakia. In Poland, 4 million Germans had been fleeing westwards since the Soviet army had begun its approach and, after **liberation**, millions more were **deported** and about 2 million died in the process. In order to avoid the Soviet troops moving westwards, the Germans forced the surviving Jews in the death and concentration camps to march some or all of the way to Germany. About a hundred thousand Jews died on these "death marches." Those still alive at the end of their journey were left in camps in Germany, where they were found in a terrible state by horrified Allied troops.

A UK soldier listens to the horror stories of the Belsen concentration camp from a liberated survivor, 1945.

# Hiroshima and Nagasaki

After the capture of Iwo Jima and Okinawa, where United States losses were greater than those in the D-Day invasion of Europe, it was clear that the invasion of mainland Japan would mean another huge loss of lives. The use of a new type of bomb, which would speed up Japan's surrender, was greeted with general relief.

The world's first atom bomb was dropped on the city of Hiroshima, Japan, shortly before 9 a.m. on 6 August 1945. In the time it took for the bomb to fall, the plane that carried it, the US *Enola Gay*, was nearly 12 miles (19 kilometres) away. Even then, one of the pilots recalled, the frame of the aircraft "crackled and crinkled" with the blast and light filled the cockpit. Three days later, a second atom bomb was dropped on the city of Nagasaki. Five days afterwards, the emperor of Japan announced by radio to his people that Japan had surrendered and the Second World War was finally over.

## Hiroshima and Nagasaki

Date: 6 August 1945
Target of atom bomb: Hiroshima
    city, population: 350,000
Type of atom bomb: Uranium
Bomb's nickname: "Little Boy"
People killed: 140,000.

Date: 9 August 1945
Target of atom bomb: Nagasaki
    city, population: 270,000
Type of atom bomb: Plutonium
Bomb's nickname: "Fat Man"
People killed: 74,000.

Many thousands more died in the days, months and years after the bombings from the effects of **radiation**.

The US *Enola Gay* was the airplane that dropped the atom bomb on Hiroshima.

# Technology and war

Great efforts were made by the warring countries to develop weapons that would give them an advantage over their enemies. Some of the most important new technologies, such as the jet aircraft, were developed by Germany. The single most important weapon, however, was developed by the United States and was used to bomb Hiroshima and Nagasaki.

## The Manhattan Project

It was the thought that Nazi Germany might develop an atom bomb that made the United States want to be the first to have the new weapon. Scientists had a good idea how destructive such a bomb would be. It would be more powerful than anything ever previously thought possible, yet the **plutonium core** of the bomb was about the

size of an orange. The secret project in the United States to develop the bomb, called the Manhattan Project, was based at Los Alamos in New Mexico. Over 50,000 people were employed there.

An aerial view of the Los Alamos Scientific Laboratory in New Mexico, where the secret Manhattan Project was based.

## The ball-point pen

Not all the new technologies developed during the war were designed to kill and destroy. Before the invention of the ball point, people wrote with pens that had to be filled with ink by hand. Known as fountain pens, they put wet ink directly on to the page and special blotting paper was used to soak up spare surface ink. In 1943, two Hungarian brothers invented a new type of pen that did not need filling. These pens were first made for RAF pilots because pressure changes in flight meant that fountain pens frequently leaked.

# Was the atom bomb necessary?

Using the atom bomb will probably remain the most controversial issue of the whole war, though at the time the reason for its use seemed clear-cut. Germany had surrendered by the time the bomb was ready to use, but Japan was still fighting. It was estimated that between 25,000 and 46,000 Americans might die if they went ahead and invaded the Japanese mainland. The bombing of the civilians of Hiroshima and Nagasaki saved these lives and those of the Japanese who would have died defending their country.

President Truman and some of the key Manhattan Project scientists, however, did not want the new weapon used to kill massive numbers of civilians. It has been argued that Japan could have been persuaded to surrender without using the bomb. Japanese leaders knew they were defeated and attempts to negotiate a peace had already begun. It has also been said that the United States wanted to use their new weapon to show the USSR how powerful it was. The United States knew that once the war was over, the USSR and itself would be the world's superpowers. If they were going to argue over control of the post-war world then, it is argued, the United States wanted to show the power they possessed.

Hiroshima, Japan, was destroyed when the atom bomb was dropped by the United States, on 6 August 1945.

# The end of an era

The period between 1936, when the Olympic Games were held in Nazi Germany, and 1945 when the atom bomb was dropped on Hiroshima, was dominated by the Second World War. It was the first war to be fought on a truly global scale and one where far more civilians than soldiers suffered and died.

The human cost of the war can be told in statistics – at least 50 million died. The suffering that people went through can only be suggested by those who survived. Dov Levin, whose parents and sister were victims of the Holocaust, wondered "Who will release us from the pain in our hearts, from the loneliness, from our memories...?"

Levin, who escaped from a ghetto and joined a Jewish resistance group, was lucky to avoid being gassed to death in a death camp. The Holocaust remains the single most awful episode in the war. The war became an instrument for terrible racial conflict: Nazis deciding Jews, Slavs, and other groups were unworthy to live, and Japanese soldiers being taught to treat the Chinese as their racial inferiors.

US soldiers wait for orders as they land in northern France on D-Day, 6 June 1944.

Soldiers and civilians on all sides, not just the Germans and Japanese, experienced the horror of war. A group of battle-weary US soldiers were asked by a journalist towards the end of the war in Europe what they would like best from back home at that particular moment. The question was greeted by a silence, until one of them replied: "Tell them it's too damned serious over here to be talking about hot dogs and baked beans and things we're missing. Tell them...there are men getting killed and wounded every minute, and they're miserable and they're suffering. Tell them it's a matter more serious than they'll ever be able to understand...that's all. That's all."

## Madness

Hitler killed himself on 30 April 1945. It took over a week for the news to reach a group of German soldiers held in a prison camp in France. One of the prisoners of war (PoW), Joachim Fest, remembers standing in front of a notice board on which the news of Hitler's suicide was posted:

"Someone said, with a sigh: 'Thank God, he's dead, and the war's over.' Others disagreed: 'How can you say that? It's the Führer! [leader].' Then an older soldier came along, hands in his pockets, and quite lax in his manner: 'Stop quarrelling,' he told the young PoWs. 'It was madness...It was madness right from the start.' This set the tone, and the crowd dissolved."

(FROM THE *INDEPENDENT*, 30 APRIL 2004)

A mother and her children pass by the battle ruins of Berlin on the way to school in October 1945. The boys carry their shoes to save on wear and tear.

# TIMELINE

**1934**

Leni Riefenstahl directs the film *Triumph of the Will*

**1935**

Hitler announces the size of the new German army (500,000)

Malcolm Campbell sets a new land speed record

**1936**

Olympic Games in Berlin, Germany

German troops occupy the Rhineland

Civil war breaks out in Spain

**1937**

Japanese troops invade China

**1938**

Hitler takes over the Sudetenland area of Czechoslovakia

**1939**

Germany invades Poland (1 September)

The UK and France declare war on Germany (3 September)

**1940**

Construction of Auschwitz death camp begins in Poland (21 February)

Denmark, Norway, the Netherlands, Belgium, Luxembourg, and France conquered by Germany (April – June)

Evacuation of UK troops from France at Dunkirk (May – June)

Battle of Britain (July – September)

German bombing campaign against British cities (the Blitz) begins (September)

United States announces oil **embargo** against Japan; UK and the Netherlands do the same

**1941**

Lend-Lease Act signed between United States and UK (March)

German invasion of the USSR begins (22 June)

German advance on Moscow is halted (November)

United States freezes all Japanese assets (26 July)

Japanese troops land in Malaya and Thailand, and Pearl Harbor attacked (7 December)

Australia and New Zealand declare war on Japan (9 December)

Hitler declares war on United States (11 December)

Japan invades Netherlands East Indies (Indonesia) (20 December)

## 1942

Siege of Bataan begins (7 January)
Singapore surrenders to the Japanese
(15 February)
General MacArthur leaves Philippines
for Australia (11 March)
US and Philippino troops surrender
on Bataan (9 April)
Battle of the Coral Sea (4–8 May)
Battle of Midway (3–6 June)
Naval battle of Guadalcanal begins
(12–13 November)
US troops land on New Georgia
(20 June)
Battle of Stalingrad begins
(25 August)
Soviet counter-attack at Stalingrad;
German troops are surrounded
(19 November)
US landings on Tarawa
(20 November)

## 1943

Start of the Battle of Kursk (5 July)
Allied landings in southern Italy
(10 July)
Roosevelt, Churchill, and Stalin
meet to discuss the war

## 1944

Leningrad siege is ended by the
Soviets (27 January)
D-Day landings in Normandy
(6 June)
Battle of the Philippine Sea
(19 June)
US landings on Guam and Tinian
(21–24 July)
The first V-2 rocket bomb lands in
the UK (8 September)
The first *kamikaze* missions, against
US escort carriers in the Battle of
Leyte Gulf (23–26 October)

## 1945

Allied bombing raid destroys
German city of Dresden
(13–14 February)
US forces land on Japanese island
of Iwo Jima (19 February)
US troops land on Japanese island
of Okinawa (1 April)
Berlin falls to the Soviet army
(30 April)
Germany surrenders to the Allies
(7 May)
VE (Victory in Europe) Day (8 May)
Atom bombs dropped on Hiroshima
(6 August) and Nagasaki
(9 August)
Japanese emperor broadcasts to the
country, announcing surrender
(14 August)

# FURTHER INFORMATION

## CDs

*Eyewitness: The 1920s* (BBC Audiobooks, 2004)
*Eyewitness: The 1930s* (BBC Audiobooks, 2004)

## Books

*Armies of the Past: Going to War in World War II,* Moira Butterfield (Franklin Watts, 2001)
*Heinemann Profiles: Anne Frank,* Sean Connolly (Heinemann Library, 1998)
*Hitler's Rise to Power and the Holocaust,* Linda Jacobs Altman (Enslow, 2003)
*Teen Witnesses to the Holocaust: In the Camps,* Toby Axelrod (Rosen, 1999)
*20th Century Media: 1940s & 50s: The Power of Propaganda,* Steve Parker (Heinemann Library, 2002)
*20th Century Perspectives: The Causes of World War II,* Paul Dowswell (Heinemann Library, 2002)
*20th Century Science & Technology: 1920–40: Science for the People,* Steve Parker (Heinemann Library, 2001)
*Witness to History: Hiroshima,* Nick Harris (Heinemann Library, 2004)
*Witness to History: The D-Day Landings,* Sean Connolly (Heinemann Library, 2003)

## Websites

http://www.ushmm.org/
United States Holocaust Memorial Museum.

http://www.holocaust-history.org/
Holocaust History Project.

www.historyplace.com
Click on the Second World War tab for interesting photographs, a timeline, and features on Pearl Harbor and African Americans in the war.

http://search.eb.com/normandy/
Find out about D-Day.

## Disclaimer

All the internet addresses (URLs) given in this book were valid at the time of going to press. However, due to the dynamic nature of the Internet, some addresses may have changed, or sites may have ceased to exist since publication. While the author and publishers regret any inconvenience this may cause readers, no responsibility for any such changes can be accepted by either the author or the publishers.

## the mid 1930s to 1945

| | |
|---|---|
| **Art and architecture** | • British artist David Hockney is born<br>• The first "pre-fabricated" houses are built in the UK. They are made out of steel and can be erected in a few hours. |
| **Books and literature** | • The first inexpensive paperback books are sold at the beginning of the 1930s<br>• *Gone With the Wind* by Margaret Mitchell (1936)<br>• *Of Mice and Men* by John Steinbeck (1937) |
| **Education** | • In the UK, the school leaving age is raised to 15 years old |
| **Fads and fashions** | • The "Slinky" toy is invented in 1945 |
| **Historic events** | • The first digital computer, named ENIAC, is completed in 1945. It weighs 30 tons (30,000 kilograms) and stands 2 stories high.<br>• The German airship Hindenburg explodes over New Jersey, United States, killing 33 passengers and crew in 1937 |
| **Music, film, and theatre** | • Big Bands, such as Glenn Miller's band, dominate popular music<br>• *Snow White and the Seven Dwarfs* is the first full-length animated film, released in 1937 |
| **People** | • British poet and writer Rudyard Kipling dies in 1936<br>• French fashion designer Yves Saint Laurent is born in 1936 |

# GLOSSARY

**Allies** countries at war against Germany, Japan, and their supporters

**ally** people or a group who are on your side

**anti-Semitism** hatred of Jewish people

**assassinate** to deliberately target and kill someone

**atom** building block of all matter

**atomic bomb** weapon of mass destruction, releasing an atom's energy

**Axis powers** countries at war with the United States, the UK, and their supporters

**bayonet** stabbing blade attached to the end of a rifle

**boycott** refuse to have anything to do with a person or a group as a form of protest

**cannibalism** eating of human flesh

**capitalist** someone who believes in an economy based on private ownership and profit

**civil war** a war taking place within a country, not against a foreign country

**colony** country ruled over by another country as part of an empire

**Commonwealth** friendly group of countries once part of the British Empire

**communism** belief that all property should be owned by the government and that each person should be paid according to their needs

**communist** person who believes in organizing ownership and spending wealth

**concentration camp** prison camp where people are forced to live

**conscript** call up into the armed forces

**death camps** Nazi-run camps in Poland where Jews and other minorities were murdered on a large scale

**defence treaty** treaty made between two or more countries in which they promise to help each other if one side is attacked

**demilitarized** without the presence of military forces

**demoralize** make to feel that there is little hope

**deported** expelled from a country or region

**dictator** single ruler with all the power

**discrimination** making a choice on the basis of, for example, race or religion

**economy** matters to do with money

**embargo** ban on trade of something with another country

**empire** control of other countries by a dominant power

**evacuate** remove from one place to live somewhere else

**ghetto** fenced-off area of a town where a certain group of people are forced to live

**Great Depression** following the Wall Street Crash, when industries all over the world went out of business and millions of people were unemployed

**internationalism** policy of co-operation between countries

**kamikaze** Japanese suicide pilots in the Second World War attacking enemy ships

**liberation** made free, released from imprisonment or very harsh conditions

**merchant ship** ship used for carrying non-military goods, like food or oil

**migrate** to travel, often from one country to another, in order to find work

**nationalist** person with a strong belief in the value of the nation to which they belong

**natural resources** valuable parts of a country's land and seas, supplies of oil or gold for example

**Nazism** racist, nationalist system of the Nazi Party that ruled Germany under Hitler between 1933 and 1945

**persecute** attack someone over an extended period of time

**plutonium core** inner part of an atom bomb

**propaganda** information that presents only one point of view

**radiation** powerful and often dangerous waves of light coming from certain materials

**ration** restrict the supply of scarce items, usually food, so that each person only receives a small amount

**raw material** basic product, like iron or oil for example, used in the manufacture of other products

**Red Army** army of the USSR

**socialism** the belief that life would be better if organized around the needs of people rather than the making of money and profits

**socialist** person who believes in equality and a fairer distribution of wealth

**social revolution** sudden and far-reaching change in the way a society is organized

**solidarity** support people show when working together

**Soviet** having to do with the USSR

**suburbs** area on the fringes of a city

**streamlining** making more efficient and cutting out waste

**swastika** symbol of Nazi Germany

**territory** land belonging to someone

**totalitarian** having complete power over other people

**trade union** organization formed by workers to protect their interests

**Treaty of Versailles** peace agreement made after the First World War

**USSR** Union of Soviet Socialist Republics

**Vichy France** French state of 1940–1944, which was a puppet government under Nazi influence

**Wall Street Crash** sudden and severe fall in the price of shares in the New York Stock Market in 1929

# INDEX